Contents

In pursuit of gold

Footballers dream of scoring the winning goal in a football World Cup. Singers hope to release a hit record and actors dream of winning an Oscar. For many sportsmen and women, their ultimate dream is to stand on the winners' **podium** at the Olympic Games and accept a gold medal that tells the world they are an Olympic champion.

The ultimate prize

The Olympics take place in a different world city every four years. It is at these spectacular events that Olympic champions take home not only a gold medal, but the satisfaction of knowing they are the best in their sport. In 2012, the Games will be held in London, UK, and the world's athletes will compete once more to become an Olympic champion.

" I stand on the podium and have them put a gold medal around my neck. US runner and Olympic medallist Michael Johnson's response when asked if he had an Olympic ritual "

Jamaican sprinter Veronica Campbell-Brown (centre) won the 200 metres with a time of 21.74 seconds at the 2008 Olympics.

The
Olympics

Larbert Library
Tel: 503590

Olympic Champions

Nick Hunter

WAYLAND

First published in 2011 by Wayland

Copyright © Wayland 2011

This paperback edition published in 2012 by Wayland.

Wayland
338 Euston Road
London NW1 3BH

Wayland Australia
Level 17/207 Kent Street
Sydney, NSW 2000

Produced for Wayland by Calcium
Design: Simon Borrough and Paul Myerscough
Editor: Sarah Eason
Editor for Wayland: Katie Woolley
Picture researcher: Susannah Jayes

British Library Cataloguing in Publication Data

Hunter, Nick.
   Olympic champions. — (The Olympics)
   1. Olympic Games (30th : 2012 : London, England)—
   Juvenile literature. 2. Olympics—Records—
   Juvenile literature.
   I. Title II. Series
   796.4'8'0922-dc22

ISBN: 978 0 7502 7066 3

Printed in China
Wayland is a division of Hachette Children's Books,
an Hachette UK company.
www.hachette.co.uk

Picture Acknowledgements:

Cover Main image: Shutterstock: Sportgraphic.
Inset images: Shutterstock: Johnny Lye tl, Gert Johannes
Jacobus Vrey tr, Webitect bl, Muzsy br, Spine image:
Shutterstock: Sportgraphic. Back cover image:
Shutterstock: Pete Niesen.
Pages Corbis: Patrick Durand/Sygma 29, Victor Fraile 6,
Leo Mason 12, Jason Reed 22; Dreamstime: Olga Besnard
17, Carmentianya 28, Sarah Dusautoir 1, 24, Shariff Che'
Lah 19, Bas Rabeling 11, Sportgraphic 27; Getty Images:
10, 18, 26, AFP 14–15, Bongarts 8, Sports Illustrated 4–5,
20; London 2012: 23; Shutterstock: cjpdesigns 2, 16, Pete
Niesen 5, Sportgraphic 9, Testing 13, Anke van Wyk 21;
Xiaming 25; Ruud Zwart: 30.

What makes an Olympic champion?

Athletes need determination and the will to win to achieve an Olympic medal, but they must also train extremely hard to become fit enough to compete at the Games. On average, athletes spend eight hours a day, seven days a week, in training to become Olympic-fit. This means they do not have time for a full-time job, so rely instead on **sponsorship** to provide the money they need to live and to pay for the team of coaches, **nutritionists**, **sports psychologists** and **physiotherapists** required to shape them into a champion.

Russia's Yelena Isinbayeva celebrates her win at the 2008 Games. The champion pole vaulter has set 27 world records and is the first woman to ever jump over five metres.

Olympics by numbers

14 Olympic gold medals have been awarded to US swimmer Michael Phelps. He will be looking for more in 2012!

18 medals were won by gymnast Larisa Latynina – the world record for Olympic medal wins by one athlete

Lightning fast: Usain Bolt

Usain Bolt looked totally relaxed as he lined up with the other athletes for the men's 100 metres final at the Beijing Olympics in 2008. The race was expected to be close between Bolt, fellow Jamaican Asafa Powell and the American Tyson Gay. In the end it was no contest: Bolt pulled away from his **rivals** to win in a record-breaking time of 9.69 seconds. He even found time to slow down and start celebrating before crossing the finish line!

Olympic insights

Bolt is six feet and five inches tall and his incredibly long legs mean he can cover seven feet in just one stride. As a result, Bolt can run 100 metres in just 41 steps – five less than any other athlete!

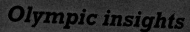

Bolt, wearing the Jamaican flag, celebrates his 2008 100-metre win by showing off the golden trainers designed by his sponsor, Puma.

Early life

Bolt was born and brought up in the Trelawny parish of Jamaica. While Bolt was playing cricket as a teenager, his coach spotted his incredible running ability and encouraged him to take up athletics.

Bolt began to train under the guidance of former Olympic sprinter Pablo McNeil, and by 2001 he had won his first medal, taking the silver in the 200-metre sprint at the high school championships in Jamaica. Then, in 2002, at the world junior championships, Bolt became the youngest-ever contestant to win a gold medal in the 200-metre race. He was just 15 years old.

Olympic sensation

In 2004, Bolt entered the Athens Olympics, but his hopes were dashed when he injured his leg and was unable to continue in the Games. Determined to make a comeback, Bolt returned to the Olympics in 2008, where he astonished **spectators** with his seemingly effortless 100-metre sprint win. He followed this with another gold medal and world record in the 200 metres. His sensational wins inspired the Jamaican team, who then went on to claim gold in the men's 4 x 100-metre relay.

What next?

Since the Beijing Games in 2008, Bolt has become one of the world's most famous athletes. He will return to the Olympic stage once more in 2012 at the London Games, where he will try to improve upon the lightning-fast wins that brought him to the world's attention in Beijing in 2008.

The all-rounder: Jessica Ennis

Heptathlete Jessica Ennis spent most of the 2008 Beijing Olympics **recuperating** at home in the UK. She should have been competing in the gruelling heptathlon event at her first Olympics but was unable to take part because of an ankle injury. Despite never having been to the Olympics, the world champion is one of the greatest female heptathletes in the world and a favourite to win gold in London in 2012.

Despite being just five feet and five inches tall, in 2007 Ennis managed to jump 1.95 metres at the International Association of Athletics Federation (IAAF) Combined Events Challenge in Italy.

> "I burst out crying... I thought it was my year to shine and do well. In the blink of an eye it was over. It was heartbreaking.
> Jessica Ennis, talking about her failure to compete at the 2008 Games because of her injury.

The toughest event

Heptathletes compete in seven different events including the 100-metre hurdles, 200-metre sprint, 800-metre race, high jump, long jump, shot put and javelin throwing events. The events take place over two days and athletes must excel in all seven track and field disciplines to win gold. Like its equivalent for male athletes, the **decathlon**, the heptathlon places huge strain on the whole body and injuries among heptathletes are common.

Ennis' small frame is unusual for her sport — most heptathletes are tall and powerful, like Tia Hellebaut (left) of Belgium.

Becoming a champion

Jessica Ennis was born in Sheffield, England, where she still lives. Jessica's parents introduced her to athletics as a teenager when they were looking for something to keep her busy during the school holidays. Little did they know that she would go on to become a world champion in so many different events.

Star stats
name: *Jessica Ennis*
date of birth: *28 January 1986*
nationality: *British*
sporting achievements:
world championships, 2009 – heptathlon champion;
*world indoor championships, 2010 – **pentathlon** champion;*
European championships, 2010 – heptathlon champion

The one to beat

When Jessica achieved her personal best high jump of 1.95 metres she jumped 30 centimetres more than her own height! This is something that only 10 female athletes have ever achieved, and Jessica has also jumped higher than any other British woman in history. Since becoming world champion in 2009, she has established herself as the athlete to beat in the women's heptathlon and is determined that in 2012 she will take home an Olympic gold.

Long-distance legend: Tirunesh Dibaba

Tirunesh Dibaba is known as 'the baby-faced destroyer' because despite looking so young, the runner has a formidable sprint finish that can destroy her challengers in the final stages of a 10,000-metre race. Tirunesh established herself as the one to watch at the 2012 Olympics in London when she won gold in the 5,000 and 10,000 metres at the Beijing Olympics in 2008.

Star stats
name: Tirunesh Dibaba
date of birth: 1 June 1985
nationality: Ethiopian
sporting achievements:
Beijing, 2008 – gold in 5,000 metres and 10,000 metres;
Athens, 2004 – bronze in 5,000 metres

Dibaba raises her hand in triumph as she takes gold in the 10,000 metres in 2008.

Born to run

Tirunesh was born in an Ethiopian village, in Africa, in 1985. She comes from a family of runners – her elder sister, Ejegayehu, won a silver medal in the 10,000 metres in Athens in 2004 and her cousin, Derartu Tulu, won two Olympic gold medals in the 10,000 metres in Barcelona in 1992 and Sydney in 2000.

Baby-faced winner

From an early age, Tirunesh showed an athletic ability similar to that of her relatives and she began competing in local athletic competitions at the age of 14. She was just 17 years old when she won her first world championship in 2003, taking the gold in the 5,000 metres. When she claimed a bronze medal in the same-distance race in Athens in 2004, she was just 19 years old, and the youngest Ethiopian to ever win an Olympic medal.

Taking London

In 2012, when the London Olympics take place, Tirunesh will be 27 years old and in her athletic prime. Few people doubt that the 'baby-faced destroyer' will be crowned an Olympic champion again.

Gebrselassie hopes to win the 2012 Olympic **marathon** in London to claim his third Olympic gold medal.

Olympic insights

Tirunesh can look forward to a long career if she follows in the footsteps of legendary long-distance runner Haile Gebrselassie. In 2012, he will be 39 years old and at an age when most athletes are thinking about **retirement**. However, he was persuaded not to retire by his fans in Ethiopia and will compete at the 2012 Games –16 years after he won his first Olympic gold medal in 1996 in Atlanta, USA.

Cycling star: Victoria Pendleton

British cyclists dominated the **track cycling** events at the Beijing Olympics, winning seven of the 10 gold medals on offer. Victoria Pendleton won the 200-metre sprint event in Beijing and will be hoping to do even better in London, where there will be more women's cycling events. Pendleton will race in the sprint, team sprint and keirin events in the 2012 Games.

Cycling as a child

During her childhood, Victoria and her twin brother, Alex, were encouraged by their father Max to race on grass cycling tracks. Max, a former grass track cycling champion, recognised his daughter's potential and entered Victoria in her first grass track race when she was just nine years old! Victoria carried on cycling throughout her teenage years, but didn't start training seriously until she went to university, where she was inspired by British cyclist Jason Queally, who won gold at the Sydney Olympics in 2000.

Star stats
name: *Victoria Pendleton*
date of birth: *24 September 1980*
nationality: *British*
sporting achievements:
Beijing, 2008 – gold in 200-metre sprint; world championships, 2010 – sprint world champion

Victoria is not as powerfully built as most cyclists, but has exceptionally strong thigh muscles. The young star took the gold in the women's individual sprint event at the Beijing Olympics.

"They're probably more worried about me, which is a comforting thought! Victoria Pendleton, speaking about the competitors she will meet at the 2012 London Olympics.

A world-class winner

After a disappointing visit to the Olympics in 2004, Victoria won her first world championship in 2005. She continued to win a medal in each world championship over the next five years, culminating in her fifth world championship title in 2010.

Training for the track

To have a chance of winning in London, Victoria has to keep up a tough training regime. A typical training day includes spending the morning in the gym weight-training to build strength, followed by three hours on the bike in the afternoon, alternating between 90 minute long-distance sessions and 100-metre sprints.

Olympic insights

Many of Britain's cyclists who won medals in Beijing will be competing again in London. Sir Chris Hoy won three gold medals in Beijing but changes to the cycling events mean that he will have fewer races in which to win gold in London. Other contenders include Ed Clancy and Nicole Cooke, who won both cycling race golds in Beijing. British track cyclists will not expect to have things all their own way in London, especially as new rules mean that only one cyclist from each country can feature in any event.

In 2012, Victoria will once more face rivals such as Vera Koedooder of the Netherlands, who beat her during the women's final at the **Union Cycliste Internationale (UCI)** championships in Beijing in 2010.

WORD FILE

keirin: an event in which cyclists draw lots to decide in which position they will start the race

peloton: a group of cyclists who 'bunch' together during a road cycling event

Golden rower: Tom James

Not only did the British dominate cycling at
the Beijing Olympics, they also excelled in
the rowing events. 'Team GB' brought
home six medals – two golds, two silvers and two bronze
rowing medals! One of the golds Britain took was in
the men's **four rowing race**, in which Tom James, along
with fellow crew members Steve Williams, Andrew Triggs
Hodge and Pete Reed, rowed to victory. The race finished
dramatically, with the British beating rivals Australia by
just 1.28 seconds. Tom hopes to repeat his outstanding
performance in the 2008 Games at London 2012.

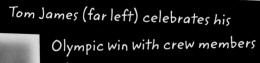

Tom James (far left) celebrates his
Olympic win with crew members
Steve Williams, Pete Reed
and Andrew Triggs Hodge.

The runner turned rower

Tom first started rowing at school in Chester, UK, after a knee injury forced him to give up running. Rowing placed less strain on his knee and Tom also quickly discovered that he had a natural talent for the sport. In 2001, when he was just 17, he competed in the men's junior **eight rowing race** in Duisberg, Germany, and won the bronze medal.

University days

In 2002, Tom went to Cambridge University, UK, where his rowing career continued. He was chosen to race in the men's four at the world rowing junior championships, and took the silver medal. Then, in 2003, he joined the senior team and won bronze in the men's eight race.

Winning the fours again would be awesome — and hopefully a few other medals as well. Tom James, talking about his hopes for the 2012 Games.

In the same year, Tom rowed in one of the most exciting Oxford v Cambridge boat races ever – in which Oxford beat Cambridge by just 30 centimetres!

Olympics and injuries

Tom then set his sights on the 2004 Olympics in Athens, where he competed as part of the British men's eight team. After the Olympics, he decided to take a break from international rowing but still continued to row for Cambridge and in his final year at university, beat Oxford in the 2007 boat race. After university, Tom returned to competitive rowing and in early 2008, he was selected to race as part of the British team in the men's four at the World Cup. However, his medal-winning hopes were dashed when he had to pull out of the race because of injury.

Rowing to victory

Tom managed to overcome his injuries to step into the British men's four boat once more at the Beijing Games later in 2008. The race was one of the most sensational Olympic rowing events in history, and Tom and his crew put in an exceptional performance to claim the gold medal. The brilliant young rower intends to add to his medal collection when he returns to the Olympic stage in 2012.

Tennis ace: Rafael Nadal

Nadal is famous for his incredibly powerful double-handed strokes, which slam the ball over the net.

"It's unforgettable to be in the **Olympic Village** with all the **elite** athletes that we only otherwise see on television."
Rafael Nadal on his experience at the Beijing Olympics in 2008.

Two men have dominated tennis in the early twenty-first century: Switzerland's Roger Federer and Spain's Rafael Nadal. These two great players have battled to be the best in most of the world's great **tournaments**. But Nadal has won something that, so far, Federer has failed to capture – an Olympic gold medal. The player is tipped to keep his Olympic title in 2012.

Star in the making

Nadal was born and still lives on the Spanish island of Mallorca. He started playing tennis at the age of four and has been coached by his uncle Toni, a former **professional** tennis player, ever since. Rafael is right-handed, but Toni encouraged him to play left-handed to give him an advantage over right-handed opponents. When Rafael was 12 years old, the Spanish Tennis Federation suggested that he train in Barcelona. Toni refused, insisting that Rafael remain at home so that he could be with his family and continue his education at his local school.

Climbing the ranks

In 2001, Rafael joined the professional tennis tour, a world tour made up of 19 tournaments in which male tennis players compete. He soon became known for his aggressive determination on the court and his exceptional stamina, which helps him to withstand the toughest of matches. Aged 15, Rafael beat tennis legend Pat Cash in a clay-court match and was just 16 when he made it to the boys' singles semi-finals at Wimbledon in 2002.

Familiar ground

Nadal's rivalry with Federer has been part of men's tennis for many years. In 2012, Rafael will be just 26 and at the peak of his fitness, so he will be hoping to retain his Olympic title. All eyes will be on the tournament at the London 2012 Olympics, to watch these two legendary players fight for the title and Olympic gold.

Olympic insights

There is no clear favourite to win the women's tennis singles at the 2012 Olympics in London. If they appear at the Games, Venus and Serena Williams will each hope to take home the crown, but both are coming towards the end of their careers, and while they have won Olympic doubles matches, neither has won an Olympic medal in the singles. Elena Dementieva, who won the women's singles in Beijing in 2008, has retired, so, in 2012, it is likely that a rising star may be crowned.

Federer is known for his smash volleys over the net and is capable of serving the ball at a speed of 220 kilometres per hour.

Badminton's best: Lin Dan

Star stats

name: Lin Dan
date of birth:
14 October 1983
nationality: Chinese
sporting achievements:
Beijing, 2008 – gold in
men's singles

Chinese badminton player Lin Dan is seen by many as the 'David Beckham' of the Asian sporting world. He has won everything there is to win in the sport of badminton, including an Olympic gold medal in 2008. Lin is one of China's most popular athletes, and is famous for smashing the shuttlecock over the net onto the opponent's side of the court. Lin Dan is well known for his antics on the court – he likes to take off his shoes at the end of a match and throw them into the crowd!

It was tipped to be a close match, but in the end Lin Dan thrashed Lee Chong Wei at the 2008 Olympic finals.

Badminton wins

Lin Dan's parents wanted him to learn to play the piano as a child, but Lin's ambitions lay elsewhere. He chose to play badminton at the age of five and rapidly grew into an exceptional player. He has played for China's national badminton team since he was 18 years old.

Olympic insights

China won more gold medals than any other country at the Beijing Olympics in 2008. Leaders of China's Olympic team have vowed to win even more medals in London. Wang Yihan, one of the best female badminton players in the world, will be hoping to match Lin Dan's success by winning gold in the women's badminton competition. China has excelled in badminton because the government supports its badminton athletes financially. This allows them to concentrate on their sport and so achieve great success.

Lee Chong Wei will be determined to win the gold in 2012 — he has hinted that he may retire after the Games.

Lin is recognised as the best male badminton player of his age and is the only player in the world to win all major badminton titles including the world championships, Asian Games, All England Open, World Cup, Thomas Cup, Asia Championships, Surdirman Cup and the Olympic Games.

Badminton rivals

There are two great athletes at the top of men's badminton. Lin's fierce rival to be the world's best badminton player is Lee Chong Wei of Malaysia.

Lin Dan came out on top when the two met in the Olympic final in Beijing. Since then, they have battled over the number one **ranking**.

A home-crowd win

Lin Dan's win in 2008 was hugely popular with the home crowd in Beijing and was the highlight of his career. 'At that moment,' he said. 'I had realised my dream, which I had worked so long for'. He is looking forward to trying to retain his Olympic title in London. Lin Dan's huge popularity means that tickets for the badminton competition will be very hard to get hold of.

Top triathlete: Emma Snowsill

One of Australia's best medal hopes is Emma Snowsill, who will do her best to repeat the **triathlon** performance that won her a gold medal in 2008. Despite her tiny frame, Emma is a formidable **triathlete**. She completed the Beijing event with such ease that she found time to grab the Australian flag and hold it up to the crowd before finishing the race!

A rocky road

Emma Snowsill comes from the Gold Coast in Queensland, Australia. She enjoyed many sports and activities, from tennis and ballet to skiing and surfing, before discovering triathlon at 16 years old.

Snowsill has won the triathlon world championship three times, in 2003, 2005 and 2006. But her path to success has not been smooth. In 2002, when Emma was in training for the 2004 Olympics in Athens, her boyfriend and fellow triathlete was knocked over and killed by a car while out training. The event rocked Emma almost to the point of giving up her triathlon career.

Star stats
name: Emma Snowsill
date of birth: 15 June 1981
nationality: Australian
sporting achievements: Beijing, 2008 – gold in women's triathlon

Emma beat fellow Australian Emma Moffat (who won bronze) to take the gold in 2008 with a time of one hour, 58 minutes and 27 seconds.

The Gold Coast girl wins gold

Emma decided to continue with her training, but her hopes of Olympic glory were shattered in 2003 when she injured her thigh and could not enter the 2004 Games in Athens. Determined not to give up, Emma trained relentlessly for the next four years, spending up to eight hours a day swimming, road cycling and running, in order to achieve her goal of winning gold at the 2008 Games.

Since her success in Beijing, Snowsill has struggled again with injury, but she still hopes to defend her title in London in 2012, where one of her main rivals once more will be Australian and double world champion, Emma Moffat.

Olympic insights

The triathlon has been part of the Olympic Games since the 2000 Olympics in Sydney. Triathletes must compete in a 1,500-metre swim, a 40-kilometre cycle and a 10-kilometre run. The triathlon is a true test of stamina as athletes move from one event to the next without a break. The transitions between swimming, cycling and running are very important as athletes can lose or gain valuable seconds at these stages.

The 1,500-metre outdoor swim is one of the most challenging stages of the triathlon event.

WORD FILE

transition: the period of time in which athletes finish one event and start another during the triathlon

transition area: an area set aside in which athletes can change clothing and equipment during the transition from one event to another

Young diving star: Tom Daley

Just like in Athens in 2004, diving events at the Beijing Olympics were dominated by China. Few people outside Britain noticed Tom Daley, the 14-year-old diver who finished seventh in the 10-metre diving competition. Daley was unconcerned about not winning a medal in Beijing. He was in preparation for his main goal – gold at the London Olympics in 2012.

Diving in

Tom started diving aged just seven years old at a local swimming pool. His natural ability was spotted by a coach who placed him in a competitive diving group. Tom then entered the national novice championships in 2003, where he won a medal in the eight- to nine-year-olds category. In 2004, aged 10, he won the **platform event** in the national junior competition, becoming the youngest diver to win the event.

Star stats

name: Tom Daley
date of birth: 21 May 1994
nationality: British
sporting achievements: world championships, 2009 – 10-metre diving champion; European championships, 2009 – 10-metre diving champion; Commonwealth Games, 2010 – two gold medals

Despite putting on a strong performance at the 2008 Games, Tom was beaten by China's spectacular diving displays.

By 2006, Tom had become the under-18 British diving champion and in 2008, aged 14, he won the 10-metre British diving championships, making him the youngest-ever winner.

Fame and pressure

Since Beijing, Tom Daley has had to deal with the usual pressures that face many teenagers, such as sitting exams at school, while establishing himself as a real contender for that gold medal. His growing fame also caused problems, leading to bullying that forced him to move to a new school. At the same time, his father and chief supporter had to deal with a life-threatening illness that sadly resulted in his death in 2011.

Olympic insights

Daley has to combine training with school and homework. He trains in the gym and the pool for four hours every day after school. Two mornings a week he also trains for two hours before school, with another three hours training and more homework on Saturday. Going to school means that Daley cannot train as often as his older rivals, who are all full-time divers.

Winning medals

Despite the personal pressures that Tom has faced, his career has gone from strength to strength, winning European, Commonwealth and world championship medals. All that he needs now is an Olympic gold medal – and he has a good chance of winning one in London in 2012.

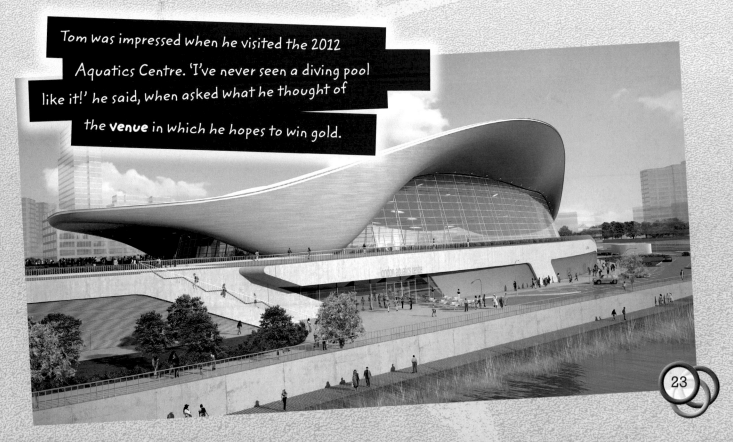

Tom was impressed when he visited the 2012 Aquatics Centre. 'I've never seen a diving pool like it!' he said, when asked what he thought of the **venue** in which he hopes to win gold.

Swimming superstars

Spectators in London in 2012 will have the chance to see one of the greatest Olympians of all time: Michael Phelps. This superstar swimmer has won a staggering 14 gold medals at the Olympics. No other Olympic athlete has won more than nine golds and Phelps will try to add to his total in 2012.

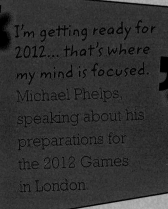

Michael spends up to eight hours a day in the pool in training for his events.

Star stats

name: Michael Phelps
date of birth: 30 June 1985
nationality: American
sporting achievements:
Athens, 2004 – six gold medals in 200-metre individual medley, 400-metre individual medley, 100- and 200-metre butterfly, 4 x 200-metre freestyle relay, 4 x 100-metre medley relay, 2 bronze medals in 200-metre freestyle and 4 x 100-metre freestyle relay; Beijing, 2008 – eight gold medals in 200-metre individual medley, 400-metre individual medley, 100- and 200-metre butterfly, 200-metre freestyle, 4 x 100-metre freestyle relay, 4 x 200-metre freestyle relay and 4 x 100-metre medley relay

"I'm getting ready for 2012... that's where my mind is focused.
Michael Phelps, speaking about his preparations for the 2012 Games in London.

Secrets of his success

Michael Phelps was born in Baltimore, USA. He was just seven years old when he started swimming in competitions. Phelps suffered from **ADHD** as a child, which made it hard for him to concentrate on one thing for long periods of time. Swimming was one area of his life where he was able to focus. Bob Bowman, who has been Phelps's coach throughout his career, soon found that Michael was not only fast but never seemed to get tired. This is essential when swimming two or three races in just a few days. This extraordinary stamina helped Michael to achieve his 14 gold medals at the Olympics.

Making a comeback

Australian swimmer and five-times Olympic gold medallist Ian Thorpe will be making a dramatic return to international swimming at the 2012 Games, after retiring in 2006. Ian intends to enter the 100-metre and 200-metre races, along with the relay events. All eyes will be on the swimmer and his rival, Michael Phelps, as they battle for the Olympic golds.

Collecting medals

Rebecca Adlington became the most successful British swimmer of all time at the 2008 Games in Beijing, taking gold in both the 400- and 800-metre freestyle events. She hopes to defend her titles in 2012, and even add a third medal to her collection by winning a gold in the relay events.

Ian Thorpe is nicknamed 'Thorpedo' because of his incredible speed in the water.

Olympic insights

There are 34 gold medals up for grabs in swimming events and Michael Phelps cannot win them all! Other swimming stars to watch in 2012 include Australian Stephanie Rice, who won three gold medals in Beijing, and Britain's double gold medallist Rebecca Adlington.

Stars of the future

One of the best things about the Games is the chance to see young athletes step onto the world stage. Athletes may be known to fans of their sport, but the Olympics can bring someone such as Usain Bolt or Victoria Pendleton to the attention of the whole world.

2012 heroes

So who might be the new stars to emerge in 2012? Here are a few possible medal-contenders:

Boaz Lalang (Kenya): this rising star of middle-distance running won gold in the 800 metres at the 2010 Commonwealth Games aged just 21.(Two other Kenyans took the silver and bronze medals.)

Liz Parnov (Australia): a young athlete who, at 17 will still be a teenager in 2012, but is making a name for herself in the pole vault event. Her father is the coach of Australia's 2008 pole vault gold medallist, Steve Hooker.

Jade Jones (see Olympic insights box) is a rising British taekwondo star who hopes to shine at the 2012 Games. She started training when she was just eight years old.

> " When I was little, my dream was to become an Olympic champion.
> Tang Yi, speaking about her hopes for the 2012 Olympics. "

Aged just 15, Tang Yi took part in the Beijing Olympics in 2008 and is tipped to take home a medal in 2012.

Francesca Halsall (Great Britain):

one of the greatest young sprint swimmers in the British team, she will be hoping to follow in the footsteps of double Olympic gold medallist Rebecca Adlington.

These possible champions of the future will inspire young people in their home countries and around the world to take up sport and possibly become Olympic champions themselves.

Olympic insights

The first **Youth Olympic Games** were held in Singapore in 2010. About 3,600 athletes between the ages of 14 and 18 competed in 26 Olympic sports. Many of the athletes who featured at the Youth Olympics may be stars of the 2012 Games.

Tang Yi: Chinese swimmer who won six gold medals.

Jade Jones: Welsh taekwondo champion who won Britain's first gold medal at the Youth Olympics.

Viktoria Komova: Russian gymnast who took home three golds and one bronze medal.

Odean Skeen: Jamaican sprinter who took gold in the 100 metres. Could he be the next Usain Bolt?

True champions

Athletes who win at the Olympics become worldwide stars. But there is more to the Olympics than winning medals and international fame. Athletes who take part in the Games are expected to follow the Olympic values – a set of guidelines designed to make the Games and the athletes who take part the very best that they can be.

Like the Olympics, the Paralympics also has its values: courage, determination, inspiration and equality.

Olympic values

Pierre de Coubertin, the founder of the 'modern-day' Olympics, established the Olympic Creed, which he believed should serve as a guideline for how the Games are conducted. It is made up of three key values:

Respect: playing fairly, knowing your limits and taking care of your health and the environment.

Excellence: giving your best (on the field and in life), taking part and progressing according to your own objectives.

Friendship: learning how to understand each other, despite any differences, through sport.

Fair play

The true champions of the Games will show these Olympic values in their performance. They will win fairly, without cheating or using illegal drugs, or by any other unfair means to gain an advantage.

The Olympic Creed

Pierre de Coubertin's Olympic Creed appears on the scoreboard at every opening ceremony. Its message reminds athletes that competing in keeping with the values is more important than the win itself – above all else, athletes should compete fairly and well.

Olympic insights

One athlete who has lived by the Olympic Creed is British athlete Derek Redmond, whose career was devastated by injuries. In 1988, he was forced to withdraw minutes before his 400-metre race at the Seoul Olympics. Again, in 1992, he reached the final in the same-distance race in Barcelona, when halfway through the race, Redmond felt his **hamstring** tear. He could no longer run, but it was his last chance at the Olympics and he was determined to finish. He hopped along the track to finish the Olympic race he had trained for all his life.

Derek's father, Jim, who had supported him throughout his career, helped Derek to finish his devastating 1992 race.

Olympic gold

Most Olympic gold medals ever won by an individual athlete:

Athlete	Olympics	Gold medals won
Michael Phelps (USA) Swimming	2004, 2008	14
Paavo Nurmi (Finland) Athletics	1920, 1924, 1928	9
Larisa Latynina (Soviet Union) Gymnastics	1956, 1960, 1964	9
Mark Spitz (USA) Swimming	1968, 1972	9
Carl Lewis (USA) Athletics	1984, 1988, 1992, 1996	9

Michael Phelps (USA) also holds the record for the most gold medals at one Olympic Games (eight golds in 2008).

Sir Steve Redgrave (Great Britain) won gold medals in rowing at five Olympic Games from 1984 to 2000 – the most consecutive victories in an endurance event.

Birgit Fischer (Germany) won gold medals in kayak events at six different Olympics between 1980 and 2004. She missed the Los Angeles Games in 1984 because East Germany did not send any athletes to those Games.

Trischa Zorn (USA) would even make Michael Phelps jealous of her achievements. This swimmer has won more medals at the Paralympics than any other. From 1980 until 2004, Zorn won 55 medals, including 41 golds, in swimming events for **visually-impaired** athletes.

Fanny Blankers-Koen (the Netherlands) won four gold medals on the track at the 1948 London Olympics. At the time, she held world records in six events but was only allowed to compete in four Olympic events. Fanny may have won more golds but the previous two Games, in 1940 and 1944, were cancelled due to the Second World War (1939–1945).

A statue in Rotterdam, the Netherlands, commemorates Fanny Blankers-Koen's Olympic achievements.

Glossary

ADHD (Attention Deficit Hyperactivity Disorder) a condition that particularly affects young people. People with ADHD have problems concentrating

decathlon an event that includes 10 different track and field disciplines

eight rowing race a rowing race in which each boat includes eight rowers

elite the best of any group

four rowing race a rowing race in which each boat includes four rowers

hamstring muscles and tendons (cords of strong fibre that attach muscles to bones) behind the knee

heptathlete an athlete that competes in the heptathlon

marathon a running race over a distance of 42.195 kilometres (26.2 miles)

nutritionists experts who advise people about what they should eat

Olympic Village specially-built accommodation for athletes and officials during the Olympics

penthathlon an event that includes five different track and field disciplines

physiotherapists experts who provide athletes with massage and exercise to heal injuries and keep them in top condition

platform event a diving event in which athletes must dive from a diving board 10-meters above the water's surface

podium a raised platform where winners are awarded medals at the Olympics

professional someone who is paid for what they do

ranking a position in a list. The athlete with the number one ranking is the best at their sport

recuperating recovering after an illness or an injury

retirement when someone stops working

rivals two people who are competing to achieve the same thing

spectators the people who watch an event happening

sponsorship to receive money from someone or an organisation in order to pursue a sport professionally. Companies may also sponsor events or people as a form of advertising

sports psychologists experts who help athletes develop a good mental attitude

tournaments sporting contests between lots of different sportspeople

track cycling bicycle racing around a steeply sloping track called a velodrome

triathlete an athlete who competes in the triathlon

triathlon an Olympic event in which athletes have to swim 1,500 metres, cycle 40 kilometres and run 10 kilometres

Union Cycliste International (UCI) championships a competition in which cyclists compete to take part at the world championships

venue a building or location where something happens. Each Olympic sport takes place in a particular venue

visually-impaired a disability affecting the eyes and a person's ability to see

Youth Olympic Games an event solely for 14 to 18-year-old athletes which is held two years after the Olympics

Further information

Books

British Olympians (21st Century Lives) by Debbie Foy (Wayland, 2009)

Great Olympic Moments (Olympics) by Michael Hurley (Raintree, 2011)

Sports Star (Celeb) by Geoff Barker (Franklin Watts, 2010)

Usain Bolt (Inspirational Lives) by Simon Hart (Wayland, 2011)

Websites

The official London Olympics site includes information about the 2012 Games and what you can expect to see there: **www.london2012.com**

The official Olympic site includes information about all Olympic medallists, including biographies and videos of great performances. Go to: **www.olympic.org/athletes**

Index